MISS JULIE

August Strindberg

English version by
Richard Nelson

BROADWAY PLAY PUBLISHING INC
224 E 62nd St, NY, NY 10065
www.broadwayplaypub.com
info@broadwayplaypub.com

MISS JULIE
© Copyright 2003 by Richard Nelson

First printing: September 2003
This printing: July 2016

I S B N: 978-0-88145-204-4

Book design: Marie Donovan
Copy editing, original edition: Sue Gilad
Publishing software: Adobe InDesign
Typeface: Palatino
Printed and bound in the U S A

This translation is based on English versions by Edwin Bjorkman (1912) and Edith & Warner Oland (1912).

This was commissioned by The Roundabout Theater (Todd Haimes, Artistic Director).

CHARACTERS & SETTING

MISS JULIE, *twenty-five*
JEAN, *a valet, thirty*
CHRISTINE, *a cook, thirty-five*

The play takes place on Midsummer's Eve, in the kitchen of the Count's country house.

(CHRISTINE *is at the stove, frying something.* JEAN *enters, holding a pair of boots which he drops on the floor. She turns to him.*)

JEAN: She's completely out of her mind. Miss Julie. Yet again.

CHRISTINE: So there you are.

JEAN: I was taking the Count to the station. Then I stopped by the barn for a dance. And there's herself leading the dancing with the gamekeeper. When she saw me she races over: she wants to dance with me now. And the way she dances. She is out of her mind.

CHRISTINE: She always was, though she's got worse now that she's not getting married.

JEAN: What do you make of that? He seemed nice enough, so what if he isn't rich. The ideas these people have. *(Sits at the end of the table)* And instead of visiting family with her father, she stays home with the servants.

CHRISTINE: Maybe she's embarrassed to face her family now.

JEAN: I'm sure. He wasn't as spineless as he looked, either; the fiancé. You know I saw it happen. Him leave her. They didn't see me.

CHRISTINE: You saw it?

JEAN: They were in the corral. Herself was "training" him, that's what she kept calling it. She held up her horse-whip and made him jump over it, like you do a dog. He fell twice and cut himself. The third time he pulled the whip out of her hand and broke it into little pieces. And—he was gone.

CHRISTINE: Just like that?

JEAN: Just like that. What's good to eat?

CHRISTINE: *(Serving from a pan)* Just some kidney I saved especially for you.

JEAN: *(Smells)* Excellent! My favorite. *(Feels the plate)* You didn't warm the plate.

CHRISTINE: You complain more than the Count. *(Playfully pulls his hair)*

JEAN: Stop it, I'm trying to eat.

CHRISTINE: I like to touch you.

(JEAN eats. CHRISTINE opens a bottle of beer.)

JEAN: Beer? On Midsummer's Eve? No, thank you. I can do better than that myself. *(Opens a drawer and takes out a bottle of claret with a yellow cap)* Yellow seal. Give me a glass—a good glass.

CHRISTINE: *(Returning to the stove)* I pity the woman who marries you.

JEAN: Right. You're lucky to get me. And proud of it too. *(Tastes the wine)* Not bad. Not bad at all. A little too cold. *(Warms the glass with his hands)* We bought it in Dijon. Four francs a litre, not counting the bottle. Plus duty. What is that awful smell, what are you cooking?

CHRISTINE: A witch's brew, on orders from the witch herself. For the dog.

JEAN: Watch what you say. So—she thinks you've nothing better to do on Midsummer's Eve than cook for her bitch? So Diana's sick?

CHRISTINE: Not exactly sick. She's been seen with the gatekeeper's mongrel. Miss Julie wishes to kill off what "trouble" may be growing.

JEAN: The young lady cares too much about some things and not enough about others. Her mother was the same way: lived in the kitchen, milked the cows, but a *single* horse for her carriage?! That wasn't good enough. She'd walk around in a filthy blouse, which had only the finest buttons. And as for the young lady, she should learn some manners. Just now in the barn she literally pulled the gamekeeper out of Ann's arm and asked him to dance. She thinks that's how we behave. It was vulgar. But she's a good-looking woman. Those shoulders and—and the rest of her.

CHRISTINE: Clara dresses her. And Clara's not impressed.

JEAN: Clara's a woman. I've been riding with her. And we've danced.

CHRISTINE: And when I'm done here, maybe you'll dance with me.

JEAN: Of course I will.

CHRISTINE: Promise?

JEAN: I said I would and I will. Thank you for supper— it was excellent.

(JEAN *pushes the cork back in the bottle with a bang.* MISS JULIE *appears in the doorway, speaking to someone outside.*)

JULIE: Be right back! Go back and dance!

(JEAN *slips the bottle back into the drawer and rises respectfully.* JULIE *goes to* CHRISTINE.)

JULIE: Are you finished?

(CHRISTINE *gestures that* JEAN *is there.*)

JEAN: *(Gallantly)* Secrets between ladies. I understand.

JULIE: *(Flaps her handkerchief in his face)* Mister Nosey!

JEAN: *(Smelling the handkerchief)* How sweet that smells.

JULIE: *(Coquettishly)* The nerve! So now you think you know something about perfumes. And your dancing's pretty good. Now don't peep! Get away.

JEAN: My guess it's a witch's broth you ladies are brewing for Midsummer's Eve—one drop and you'll see the face of your intended in the stars.

JULIE: My eyes aren't that good. *(To* CHRISTINE*)* Bottle some and cork it. *(To* JEAN*)* And you come and dance with me.

JEAN: Forgive me, but I've promised the next dance to Christine.

JULIE: She can find someone else. Can't you? Come on, let me borrow him.

CHRISTINE: If it's what Miss Julie wants, how can I refuse her? *(To* JEAN*)* Go, and be thankful for such an honor.

JEAN: To be bold, is it wise to be seen dancing so much with one man? People do talk.

JULIE: And say what? What do you mean?

JEAN: Don't you know? I'll be even bolder then: it looks curious to prefer one servant over all the others when each hopes to have the same unusual honor bestowed upon him.

JULIE: Prefer? Don't be ridiculous! Don't be silly! I, the mistress of this house, deign to honor this dance with my presence, and when it so happens that I do want to dance, I want to dance with someone who knows how to dance, so I don't end up flat on my face.

JEAN: As you wish. I'm here to serve.

JULIE: I'm not ordering you. Tonight we're all just happy people—no orders. Give me your arm. Don't worry, Christine, I'll bring him back.

(JEAN *offers his arm and they go off.*)

(Pantomime)

(CHRISTINE *is alone. Music is heard in the distance. She begins to hum the tune as she clears off the table. She wipes the plate clean, and puts it away in the cupboard. She takes off her apron, takes out a small mirror from a table drawer and leans it against the vase on the table. She lights a candle and heats a hairpin, which she uses to curl her front hair. She goes to the door and stands listening. She comes back to the table. She notices the handkerchief* JULIE *left, picks it up, smells it, spreads it out absent-mindedly and begins to stretch it, smooth it, fold it.* JEAN *returns alone.*)

JEAN: Out of her mind. She is out of her mind. The way she dances. And they're all laughing behind her back. What do you make of her?

CHRISTINE: She's getting her period. And that always makes her odd. Now are you going to dance with me or not?

JEAN: Then you forgive me for—.

CHRISTINE: What's to forgive? I know my place.

JEAN: You are a practical girl. You'll make a good wife. *(He puts his arm around her waist.)*

JULIE: *(Enters, and surprised by what she sees)* Fine partner you are—running away.

JEAN: Only to return to the one I deserted.

JULIE: *(Changing tone)* Do you know, there's nobody that dances like you! Why are you still in uniform? Take it off.

JEAN: Then please step outside. My coat is hanging right there. *(Points to his coat and goes to it)*

JULIE: Shy? In front of me? You're just changing coats. Do it in your room then. Or do it here and I'll cover my eyes.

JEAN: Excuse me. *(He goes off. One arm can be seen as he changes coats.)*

JULIE: Are you and Jean engaged? Is that what's going on?

CHRISTINE: I suppose so. In a way. Yes.

JULIE: In what way?

CHRISTINE: Well, didn't you have a man of your own, and—.

JULIE: We were officially engaged.

CHRISTINE: And where did that get you?

(JEAN enters dressed in a black coat and derby.)

JULIE: *Tres gentil, Monsieur Jean! Tres gentil.*

JEAN: *Vous voulez plaisanter, Madame!*

JULIE: *Et vous voulez parler francais!* Where did you learn that?

JEAN: Switzerland. I worked as a butler in a big hotel in Lucerne.

JULIE: You look like a real gentleman in that. Not bad. *(She sits at the table.)*

JEAN: You flatter me.

JULIE: Why would I flatter you?

JEAN: I know I do not look like a real gentleman in this, so I assume you are exaggerating which is the definition of flattery.

JULIE: And where'd you learn to talk like that? Do you go to the theatre a lot?

JEAN: There. And many other places.

JULIE: But you were born right near here?

JEAN: My father was a cotter on the county attorney's property. As a child, I saw Miss Julie, but Miss Julie, I'm sure, never saw me.

JULIE: Is that true?

JEAN: Yes—there was one time that particularly sticks in the mind, but I can't talk about that.

JULIE: Do, please! When was it?

JEAN: No. Really. I can't. Maybe another time.

JULIE: Another time's like saying never. Was it so awful?

JEAN: Not awful—just difficult. Look at that one.

(JEAN *points to* CHRISTINE *who has fallen asleep on a chair by the stove.*)

JULIE: She'll make a pleasant enough wife. Probably even snores.

JEAN: She doesn't. But she talks in her sleep.

JULIE: How do you know?

JEAN: I've heard her.

(Pause)

JULIE: Sit down.

JEAN: Is that proper?

JULIE: What if I order you?

JEAN: Then I obey.

JULIE: Sit down! Wait! I'm thirsty, I want a drink.

JEAN: I think we've nothing but beer.

JULIE: You call that nothing? I have such simple tastes, I prefer it to wine.

(JEAN *takes a bottle from the icebox, opens it, gets a glass and a plate from the cupboard and serves the beer.*)

JEAN: Allow me.

JULIE: Thank you. What about for you?

JEAN: My tastes aren't so simple, but if it's an order....

JULIE: Order? For a gentleman to keep a lady company?

JEAN: Yes. That's true. *(Opens another bottle, takes out a glass)*

JULIE: Drink to my health.

(JEAN hesitates.)

JULIE: You are shy—a big man like you.

JEAN: *(Kneels and with mock seriousness, raises his glass)* To the health of her royal highness!

JULIE: I like that. Now kiss your highness's royal shoe. That's what they do, isn't it?

(JEAN hesitates, then takes hold of her foot and touches it lightly to his lips.)

JULIE: Very good. You should have been an actor.

JEAN: *(Getting up)* Now that's enough, someone's going to see us.

JULIE: So what?

JEAN: They'll talk or keep talking. I doubt if their tongues have even stopped wagging.

JULIE: What about? Tell me. Sit down!

JEAN: *(Sits)* I don't want to upset you, but they're saying—they're calling you a—they're suggesting—. You know what they're saying. You're not a child. A woman, a man alone drinking—it doesn't matter that he's only a servant. And it's night, so....

JULIE: So?? And who's alone. Christine's right there.

JEAN: But she's asleep.

JULIE: Then I'll wake her up. Christine, wake up.

(CHRISTINE *mumbles in her sleep.*)

JULIE: Christine! I've never seen such a sound sleeper.

CHRISTINE: *(Mumbling in her sleep)* I've polished the Count's boots. They're outside his door....

JULIE: *(Pinches her nose)* I said, wake up!

JEAN: Let her sleep.

JULIE: Why?

JEAN: She's a right to be tired. Standing all day in front of a stove. She has the right to sleep.

JULIE: A noble sentiment, nobly spoken. *(She gives* JEAN *her hand.)* Come and pick me some lilacs.

(During the following, CHRISTINE *wakes up. She moves, as if still asleep, and goes off to bed.)*

JEAN: With you?

JULIE: With me.

JEAN: That won't do.

JULIE: I don't understand. You can't be thinking—?

JEAN: Not me. Others.

JULIE: What? That I fancy a servant??

JEAN: I know better; but it's been known to happen, and—common people think what they want, the baser the better.

JULIE: So they're the 'common people.' What does that make you?

JEAN: Better.

JULIE: So a mistress just by choosing to be among the servants—?

JEAN: They won't see it as a choice, but as a need.

JULIE: I have a higher opinion of people than that. Let's see who's right. Come. *(She looks at him, to dare him.)*

JEAN: I don't understand you.

JULIE: No? And I don't understand you. But it's the same for everything. Life, men, everything—flotsam and jetsam bobbing on the water until it sinks. That reminds me of a dream I keep having. I have climbed a high pillar and sit, I have no idea how to get down. Looking down makes me dizzy, but I must get off. I'm scared to jump. I start to slip, I long to fall, but I don't. I can't rest until I'm off this pillar, until I'm down, down. And should I reach the ground, I know I'd want to go down even more, down farther, down into the ground. Have you ever felt like that?

JEAN: No. In my dream I'm lying under a tall tree in a dark wood. I long to climb this tree, to reach the top from which I'll see a glorious countryside under a smiling sun. And rob the nest of its golden eggs. I climb and climb, but the trunk is thick and slippery, and the first branch is so high. If I can only reach that branch, the rest will be simple. I have not reached it yet, but I will, if only in my dreams.

JULIE: Listen to us babbling on about our dreams. Come on! Off to the garden!

(JULIE *offers her arm, they go toward the door.*)

JEAN: They say leave nine different kinds of flowers under your pillow on Midsummer's Eve and all your dreams, Miss Julie, will come true. (*He puts his hand to his eye.*)

JULIE: What's wrong?

JEAN: Nothing, some dirt. I'll be fine.

JULIE: It was my sleeve that rubbed against it. Sit down and let me…

(JULIE *takes* JEAN *by the arm and makes him sit. Takes ahold of his head and bends it back and tries to get the dirt out with the corner of her handkerchief*)

JULIE: Sit still, I said! *(Slaps his hand)* Why can't you do what I say? Are you shaking? A big strong man like you? *(Feels his biceps)* With arms like these?

JEAN: Miss Julie.

JULIE: Yes, Monsieur Jean.

JEAN: *Attention! Je ne suis qu' un homme.*

JULIE: Will you sit still! There, it's gone. Kiss my hand and thank me.

JEAN: *(Standing)* Miss Julie, please. Christine isn't here anymore. Please—

JULIE: Kiss my hand.

JEAN: Please!

JULIE: Kiss my hand.

JEAN: Blame only yourself then.

JULIE: For what?

JEAN: For what? You're twenty-five years old, how innocent can you be? It's dangerous to play with fire.

JULIE: Not for me. I'm insured.

JEAN: No you're not. But even if you were, there's flammable material all around.

JULIE: Meaning you.

JEAN: Yes. And not because of who I am, but what I am. A young man with—.

JULIE: Good looks? You are conceited. So Don Juan, is it? Or handsome Joseph? My God you look like my image of Joseph.

JEAN: I do?

JULIE: It's almost scary.

(JEAN goes to JULIE, grabs her around the waist to kiss her.)

JULIE: *(Hits him)* How dare you!

JEAN: Did you mean that or are you playing?

JULIE: I meant it.

JEAN: But a minute ago, you seemed to mean that too. You play too seriously. Someone could get hurt. I quit, allow me to leave and get back to my work, the Count will need his boots and it's already past midnight.

JULIE: Put those boots down.

JEAN: No, I'm hired to work, not to be your playmate. I wouldn't be a good one anyway, I have too much self-respect.

JULIE: You're proud.

JEAN: More in some things than with others.

JULIE: Have you ever been in love?

JEAN: That's not a word we use. But I've liked a lot of girls, and one time one even made me sick, because I couldn't have her. Sick: like those princes in the Arabian Nights who can't eat, drink because they love.

JULIE: Who was she? *(Silence)* Who was she?

JEAN: You won't get that out of me.

JULIE: What if I ask you as an—equal, a friend. Who was she?

JEAN: You.

JULIE: *(Sits down)* How funny.

JEAN: Yes, I suppose, it is very funny. This is the story I didn't want to tell you before. But I'll tell you now. Do you know how your world looks to mine? You don't. Like a hawk, a falcon whose back we can't even see as it soars high above us, far out of reach. I grew up in a cotter's hovel, with seven brothers and sisters, and a pig—out there on the grey plain, where there isn't even a single tree. But from our window I could see your father's garden, and the apple trees rising above the walls. That garden was Eden and I imagined it must be guarded by fierce angels and flaming swords. But angels or no angels, some boys and I found a way in, and we picked all we wanted from—the Tree of Life. Do you hate me?

JULIE: All boys steal apples.

JEAN: That's what you *say*, but you hate me. So what? Once I entered to weed the onion bed with my mother. Near the orchard stood a Turkish pavillion, shaded and covered in honeysuckle and jasmine. I didn't know what it was for, I'd never seen anything so beautiful. People went in, people went out, the door was left open. So I peeked. The walls were covered in pictures of kings, the windows had red, fringed curtains—why am I telling you? *(He breaks off a lilac sprig and holds it under her nose.)* I'd never been inside your house, never seen the inside of anything but the church and this was so much better. I became obsessed with this place and couldn't think about anything else. I had to taste its pleasures. The End. I snuck in, looked, admired. Someone was coming. There was only the one door, but like a rat I found a crack to sneak through.

(JULIE, who had taken the sprig, lets it drop on table.)

JEAN: I ran, fought my way through a raspberry hedge, trampled a strawberry bed, and found myself by the rose bushes on the terrace—which is where I saw— you: pink dress, white slippers and stockings. You. I hid in a pile of weeds—under the weeds, among stinging nettles, and my face pressed against the damp, stinking mulch. I watched you walk among the roses. And I thought: how unfair that the thief on the cross could gain entrance to Heaven, but a cotter's boy was not allowed to enter the Count's garden and play— with you.

JULIE: Do you think most poor boys have thoughts like that?

JEAN: *(Hesitates, then)* All poor boys do.

JULIE: It must be awful to be poor.

JEAN: Miss Julie! Miss Julie—a lady's dog gets to lie against her leg. Her horse is stroked by her hand. But her servant? There are exceptions, but they only prove the rule. To get back to my story: I threw myself into the cool brook, got soaked, and got a spanking. But the next Sunday, when my whole family went to visit my grandmother, I made up an excuse to stay home. I washed myself, put on my best clothes—such as they were—and went to church to find you. And there you were and all I knew was that I wanted to die. I wanted to close my eyes and die. Elderberry blossoms are poisonous. There was a big bush in full bloom. I raped it of its blossoms and out of them made a bed in the oat-bin. Have you ever noticed how smooth oats are? As smooth as human skin. I climbed in, covered myself, fell asleep. When I awoke I wasn't dead—as you can see—just very sick. What did I want? Who knows. You were beyond my reach, and just knowing this showed me how hopeless my life was going to be.

JULIE: You tell a good story. Did you go to school?

JEAN: A little. But I read, and go to the theatre. And as a servant one can't help but overhear one's betters, and that's an education in itself.

JULIE: You eavesdrop on us?

JEAN: Of course. From the coachbox, while rowing the boat. I've heard you with your girlfriends.

JULIE: And what did you hear?

JEAN: I wouldn't repeat it. But you surprised me, I wouldn't have thought you knew such words. Perhaps people aren't so different as we think, no matter what their background.

JULIE: How dare you! You think I acted like you and her when I was engaged?

JEAN: Is that so? Play the innocent, if that makes you happy.

JULIE: My engagement was a mistake.

JEAN: They always say that—afterwards.

JULIE: Always?

JEAN: Always. Those exact words: "I've made a mistake." I've heard it countless times.

JULIE: When?

JEAN: In situations like the ones we are discussing. Let's see, the last time—

JULIE: *(Getting up)* Stop it! I don't want to hear anymore.

JEAN: They always say that too. Allow me to go to bed.

JULIE: Bed? But it's Midsummer's Eve.

JEAN: The dancing horde out there doesn't interest me.

JULIE: Then get the boat key and row me out into the lake. I want to see the sunrise.

JEAN: Not a good idea.

JULIE: Afraid of what people will say?

JEAN: Why shouldn't I be? Who wants to be made a fool of? And who wants to be driven out of his job without even a reference? I can't afford that. And there's Christine, I don't want to hurt her.

JULIE: So—it's Christine.

JEAN: Yes. And you. Listen to me, go upstairs, go to bed.

JULIE: Is that an order?

JEAN: Obey it. And for your own good. Please. It's the middle of the night. No sleep can make one drunk, and the brain burn. Go to bed! Listen, they're coming to get me. If they find us here, the world will know.

CHORUS: *(Off, singing)*
Two girls in the woods I met
Thumpity Thumpity Thump
Down their legs it was all wet
Thumpity Thumpity Thump
Like them both, one girl said
Thumpity Thumpity Thump
Tom though was the best in bed
Thumpity Thumpity Thump
Fred I'll marry, she did say
Thumpity Thumpity Thump
Tom I'll keep for a rainy day
Thumpity Thumpity Thump

JULIE: They know me. They love me and I love them. Let them see us.

JEAN: They don't love you. They eat your food and spit at your back. Believe me. Don't you hear what they're singing?! No, don't listen.

JULIE: What are they singing?

JEAN: They're teasing us.

JULIE: How dare they!

JEAN: They're out there in the dark. And the dark makes people brave. They can't find us. We have to hide.

JULIE: Hide? Where? We can't go to Christine's—.

JEAN: Why not? Then my room. There's nowhere else. You can trust me, I am your friend.

JULIE: And if they look for you there?

JEAN: I'll lock the door. If they try to push it in, I'll shoot. Come. Come!

JULIE: And you won't—?

JEAN: I swear to God.

(JULIE *hurries off, followed by* JEAN. *The crowd is close, and just as it is about to burst into the kitchen.*)

(Blackout)

(As the lights come back up, we see the disorder and mess left by the crowd. JULIE *enters alone. She looks around at the mess. She takes out her powder and powders her face.* JEAN *enters.)*

JEAN: We can't stay here.

JULIE: No. What do we do?

JEAN: Run away. Far away.

JULIE: Where?

JEAN: Switzerland. The Italian lakes. Do you know it?

JULIE: *(Shakes her head)* Is it beautiful?

JEAN: Like eternal summer. Orange trees. Laurels. You won't believe your eyes.

JULIE: And what do we do there?

JEAN: I'll open a hotel. First class.

JULIE: Hotel?

JEAN: It's a good life, you'll see. Every day new faces. New languages. No time to get bored. Something to do every minute of the day: bells ring, trains arrive, buses come and go and the constant ping of your cash register. What could be better?

JULIE: For you, yes, but for me?

JEAN: My partner—my mistress. You've got the looks, you've got the class—think how you'll be treated. A queen able to charge an army of slaves with the push of an electric button. Guests paying you court and me—money. You wouldn't believe how nervous people can get when they pay their bills—I pad their bills, while you pad their egos with that sweet smile. Let's get out of here. *(Pulls a timetable out of his pocket)* Now. On the next train. We can be in Malmo by six thirty, Hamburg by eight forty in the morning, then Frankfurt, Basel, and Lake Como via Saint Gotthard—in three days. Only three days!

JULIE: That's the easy part, Jean. But I need courage. Take me in your arms and tell me you love me.

JEAN: I will. But not now. Not in this house. But I do love you. Haven't I proven that, Miss Julie?

JULIE: Julie. Call me Julie. You're not my servant anymore.

JEAN: I am as long as I'm in this house. Your father's house, a man I have the greatest respect for. I need only notice his gloves lying on a chair to make me feel like I am nothing. Or hear the bell and I'm a nervous mount out of the gate. There are his boots, my reflex is to bow and scrape to them. *(He kicks the boots.)* The habits of a lifetime aren't easily broken. Let's go to a country where they bow to free men, and free men bow to no one. I was not born a servant, I was made one. Let me reach that first branch, then watch me climb. Coachman today, this time next year, I'll own a hotel. Two years, rich. Three, I'll be the count.

JULIE: You will. You will.

JEAN: In Roumania they're selling titles cheap. I'll make you a countess. Mine.

JULIE: I don't need a title. I'm giving up a title. Just say you love me. Then I'll know who I am.

JEAN: I will. But not now, not here. Now try to control your emotions or this will never work. We need to think this through—calmly, sensibly. *(He takes out a cigar, cuts it, lights it.)* Sit there. I'll sit here. And let's talk only business as if nothing has happened.

JULIE: Have you no feelings?

JEAN: I have feelings. But I keep them under control.

JULIE: But before, you kissed—.

JEAN: That was then. This is what's important now.

JULIE: Don't talk to me like that.

JEAN: Like what? Like someone with sense? We've made enough mistakes for one day. Your father could be home any minute and before he comes I want this settled. Do you agree about the hotel?

JULIE: Fine. I agree. But one question: won't we need money?

JEAN: *(Chewing the cigar)* Money? Yes. But also experience, ability. I know different languages, I know service. I supply that.

JULIE: But that won't even buy a train ticket.

JEAN: No. For that—I need a backer who has money.

JULIE: And who might that be?

JEAN: It's the job of my partner to find one.

JULIE: I couldn't—. And I don't have any money myself.

(Pause)

JEAN: Then that's the end of that.

JULIE: And—?

JEAN: And nothing's changed.

JULIE: No! You think I'm going to live under this roof as your whore?! Everyone will know! I won't be able to look Father in the face! No, you have to take me away! Oh God, what have I done? What have I done?!! *(Cries)*

JEAN: "What have I done?" How many times have I heard that too? You've done nothing—unique, trust me.

JULIE: *(Crying)* Now you hate me. I'm falling. I'm falling.

JEAN: Fall to me. I'll lift you back up later.

JULIE: What terrible force drew me to you? That of the weak for the strong, of those falling for those climbing up? Or was it love? Was it love?!

JEAN: Love's as good a name as anything for it.

JULIE: You are so crude, your mind's in the gutter.

JEAN: I'm the way the world made me. And don't play the princess with me, I'm as good as you now. Look, girl, how about a drink, I've got a real treat here. *(Opens the drawer, takes out the wine bottle and fills two glasses that have already been used)*

JULIE: Where did you get that?

JEAN: The cellar.

JULIE: My father's Burgundy.

JEAN: Nothing's too good for a son-in-law.

JULIE: And I was willing to drink beer.

JEAN: Maybe I just have more refined tastes than you.

JULIE: Thief.

JEAN: And who are you going to tell?

JULIE: Now—accomplice to a common thief. Am I drunk or dreaming? Midsummer's Eve—as a child I loved this day.

JEAN: You're not a child anymore.

JULIE: There's no human being on earth unhappier than me.

JEAN: Why? Look what you've won. Think of poor Christine, or don't you think she even has feelings.

JULIE: I used to think so, not now. A servant is a servant.

JEAN: And a whore is a whore.

JULIE: *(Falls down)* Dear God, help me, I want to die! I am drowning in filth! Save me. Save me.

JEAN: How you've changed, I do feel sorry for you. When I was hiding in the onions, watching you among the roses, you got me so excited, in the way boys get excited. I can tell you that now.

JULIE: You said you wanted to die.

JEAN: Among the oats? Oh that was talk.

JULIE: You mean lies!

JEAN: I suppose. I'd read about some boy crawling into a wood-box full of lilacs because a girl was suing him to support her kid—.

JULIE: What kind of man are—?!

JEAN: It's what popped into my head. A romantic thought. The kind you women like.

JULIE: Damn you!

JEAN: And you.

JULIE: Now you've seen the falcon's back—.

JEAN: And on her back.

JULIE: I was to be that first branch—

JEAN: Too weak to hold me.

JULIE: The sign outside the hotel.

JEAN: And I'm the hotel.

JULIE: Sit at the desk, allure guests, overcharge them—.

JEAN: I'll do that part.

JULIE: How can a human soul get so rotten?

JEAN: Not rotten, dirty. So it'll wash off.

JULIE: You lackey, you servant, stand up when I talk to you!

JEAN: You're the lackey's love, the servant's fuck! Shut up and get out of here. What right do you have to call me vulgar?! No servant would even begin to know how to act as vulgarly as you have tonight! The way you went after me, threw yourself at me—no servant girl could sink so low. I've never seen anything like it, except with animals—or prostitutes.

JULIE: (*Crushed*) You're right. Strike me, step on me, it's what I deserve. I am what you say. But help me. Help me, there must be a way out of this.

JEAN: Still I'm too honorable a man not to accept some share of responsibility. But you can't imagine a man in my position ever daring to even look at you without— the invitation. Actually I sit here stunned—

JULIE: And proud.

JEAN: Not much. You made it too easy.

JULIE: Strike me again.

JEAN: (*Stands*) No. Rather forgive me for saying it. You are defenseless and you are still a lady. On the one hand, it pleases me to know now that I've been dazzled by fool's gold, that the falcon's back is as grey as the rest of him, that there's a smudge of powder on the tender cheek, soot under the polished nails, and that the handkerchief has been used and is dirty, while still smelling of perfume.
On the other hand, it hurts me to know now that what I sought is neither better nor more real. It hurts to see you sink so low you are beneath your own cook—it hurts as it hurts to watch fall flowers whipped by rain and turned into mud.

JULIE: You talk as if you're already better than me.

JEAN: I am. Don't you see, I could have made you a countess, but you couldn't make me a count.

JULIE: I'm the child of a count, you'll never be able to say that.

JEAN: No. But I might be the father of counts if—.

JULIE: You're a thief. And I am not.

JEAN: There are worse things than thieves. Anyway, you serve in a house, you become like a member of the family, another child almost—and a child who sneaks a few berries off a full heavy vine, is he a thief?
You are an exquisite woman—much too good for me. You got swept away for a moment, now to explain that to yourself—you have to be in love with me. But you're not. You may want me, but if that is love, you're no better than me. And I won't be satisfied being but an animal to you, I need your real love, which I'll never get.

JULIE: Are you sure?

JEAN: Why, you want to try? That I love you, there can be no doubt. You are beautiful, cultured—. *(Takes her hand)* So well brought up, and charming when you put your mind to it. You arouse in a man a heat not easily suppressed. *(Puts his arm around her waist)* Like wine, hot and spiced, and with kisses—.

(JEAN tries to lead JULIE away, she pulls gently back.)

JULIE: That's not the way.

JEAN: How then? If that's not the way? If not with caresses, if not by words? If not by forgetting who we are, and imagining who we will be? How then?

JULIE: How? I don't know. It's not possible. You repel me more than any rat. Yet I can't run away.

JEAN: Run away *with* me.

JULIE: Run away? Yes, that's what we'll do. But I'm so tired. Get me a drink.

(JEAN *pours her a glass of wine.* JULIE *looks at her watch.*)

JULIE: Let's talk first. We still have time. *(Empties her glass and holds it out for more)*

JEAN: Don't drink so much. It'll go to your head.

JULIE: So what?

JEAN: So? It's common. Talk about what?

JULIE: I'll go with you. But first we have to talk. Let me talk now—you've been doing all the talking. You've told me about your life, now I'll tell you about mine. So we'll both have bared ourselves in front of each other, before beginning our journey.

JEAN: Careful. Think before you speak. Or you might be sorry later.

JULIE: Aren't you my friend?

JEAN: Yes, when I can be. But be careful.

JULIE: You don't mean that. Anyway I have no secrets. Everyone knows about this. My mother—came from simple folk. She—wasn't the daughter of a count. She'd been brought up to believe in women's rights, equality for women, all that sort of thing. She detested the institution of marriage. And then father came along, she swore she'd never marry—then one day she did. Then there was me—an accident, I now think. And I became her experiment, taught to do everything a boy was supposed to do, told again and again that this was how God meant us to be. I was to be the Proof that Woman was just as good as Man. I was made to wear pants like a boy, taught to handle a horse, but not a cow, I was never allowed to milk a cow—that wasn't man's work. I groomed, hunted, did it all. I was even taught something about farming. And all over the farm, women servants were taking men's jobs and it was a disaster. We were nearly ruined, we were the laughingstock of the county. Father finally came to his senses, broke the spell mother had cast over him, and took charge. Then Mother got "sick"— no one knew with what, she had fits, stayed in bed for days, then sometimes stayed away all night. Then came the fire— you've heard about that. The house, stable, barn— gone. Under suspicious circumstances, as they say. It happened the day our insurance expired. The premium having been sent, but delayed by a "lazy" messenger. So—too late. *(She fills her glass and drinks.)*

JEAN: You've had enough to drink.

JULIE: So—what? We had nowhere to sleep, so we slept in the carriages. Father had nowhere to turn, then mother said, how about asking a childhood friend of hers, a brick manufacturer, living not too far from her. Father got a loan—for no interest. That confused him. The house was rebuilt. *(Drinks again)* So who set the fire?

JEAN: Your mother.

JULIE: And who was the brick manufacturer?

JEAN: Her lover?

JULIE: And whose money was loaned?

JEAN: That I don't know.

JULIE: My mother's.

JEAN: Which means it was your father's.

JULIE: She'd had it before they were married and she'd hid it from him. Her friend had been investing it for her.

JEAN: In his name.

JULIE: That's right. Eventually father figured it out. But what could he do? Sue to get his wife's money back from her lover? Where was the proof? Mother's revenge for taking over the farm. He nearly shot himself. Rumor has it he tried once and missed. He pulled himself together, and took out his anger on mother. Five years of hell I'll never forget. I felt sorry for father, but took mother's side, I didn't know any better. And at her side I learned to suspect, no—hate— men. She hated your whole sex, as you've probably heard. And I swore on her death bed that I'd never become a man's slave.

JEAN: And yet you became engaged to the county attorney.

JULIE: To make him my slave.

JEAN: But he wasn't willing.

JULIE: Oh he was willing. He just got boring.

JEAN: Bored. That's just how you looked with him in the stableyard.

JULIE: What do you mean?

JEAN: I was there when he broke off the engagement.

JULIE: That's not true! I broke it off. Did that liar say that?

JEAN: Why call him names? So, Miss Julie—you hate men.

JULIE: I do! With every ounce of my body. Though sometimes, one is weak…

JEAN: And me? You hate me?

JULIE: I hate every inch of you. I long to see you shriveled up and dead.

JEAN: Shot like a mad dog foaming at the mouth?

JULIE: Yes.

JEAN: But you don't have a gun. And I am not a mad dog. So what do we do?

JULIE: Run away together.

JEAN: And torture each other to death?

JULIE: No—so we can enjoy each other. For a couple of days, a week, for as long as we can. Then—die.

JEAN: Die?? Don't be silly. We'll open a hotel.

JULIE: *(Without listening)* On the shore of Lake Como, where the sun always shines, crowned by laurel even at Christmas, and oranges everywhere like moons.

JEAN: Como's a mud hole. It rains all the time, and the only oranges you'll see are on a fruit stand. Still it attracts tourists, especially couples who don't care if it rains. And they're the best business to be in—couples. You know why? Because they rent for six months, then leave after three weeks.

JULIE: Why after three weeks?

JEAN: They fight. But they still have to pay for the full six months. So you rent out the same place again. They come, they go. There is so much love in the world—it just doesn't last very long.

JULIE: Die with me.

JEAN: I don't want to die. Period. I like life, God's Gift should not be thrown away.

JULIE: How can *you* believe in God?

JEAN: I do and I go to church pretty much every other week. This has gotten tiring. I'm going to bed.

JULIE: And I'm to let you? You owe a woman you've just had a little more than that.

(JEAN takes out coins and throws them on the table.)

JEAN: Thank you. I pay my debts.

JULIE: *(Pretending not to notice the insult)* There's the law. What you've done is a crime.

JEAN: Pity there's no law against a woman having a man.

JULIE: *(Ignoring him)* So we what? Run away. Get married. Get divorced?

JEAN: You're not good enough for me.

JULIE: Me?

JEAN: To say nothing about your family. Thank God there are no arsonists in mine.

JULIE: Are you sure?

JEAN: No reason to think otherwise. Though we've few records—except those on file with the police. Your family history I know—I looked through the book lying on the drawing-room table. Do you know who your earliest known relative was? A miller whose wife serviced the king during the Danish war. I have no such relatives.

JULIE: This is what I get for talking about my family with someone like you.

JEAN: I did say: be careful. And: don't drink too much.

JULIE: What have I done? What have I done? If only you loved me!

JEAN: And how do I show you if I did?! For the last time—how?!! By crying? By jumping over your whip? By kissing? By luring you to Como for three weeks and then…? How?!! What do you want?! I'm so tired of this. But it's always this way with women. Miss Julie, I know you are unhappy, I know you are suffering, but I can't figure out why. Men aren't like this. We don't act like this. For one, we don't have time for it, we have our work to do! For us, love is fun, why can't it be for you?! You women are sick, sick!

JULIE: Be nice to me. I'm a human being.

JEAN: Are you? You spit on me, and then complain when I wipe it off on you.

JULIE: Help me, help me! Tell me what to do? How do I get out of this?

JEAN: I wish I knew.

JULIE: I was out of my mind, what could I have been thinking? Now what do I do?

JEAN: Stay here. Say nothing. No one knows anything.

JULIE: People know. Christine knows.

JEAN: They don't and they'll never suspect.

JULIE: *(Hesitating)* But—it might happen again.

JEAN: And it will.

JULIE: And then what?

JEAN: And then what? Why didn't I think of this? You can't stay here—you must leave. And now. I can't go with you or they'll guess. You have to go alone, go—anywhere!

JULIE: By myself? Where? I can't.

JEAN: You have to and before your father returns. If you stay, you know what will happen. Now that we've started, we won't stop. And we'll just get more and more careless about it too. Write your father—confess all—except that it was me. He'll never guess that, and probably he won't even want to know.

JULIE: I'll go only with you.

JEAN: Don't be stupid, woman! Miss Julie runs off with the butler! It'll get in the papers, think what that would do to the Count.

JULIE: I can't go. I can't stay. Help me, I feel so tired—so sleepy. Tell me what to do, order me—I can't think any more—can't move....

JEAN: Listen to you. You people are good for nothing. You strut and shout and then can't do anything! You want an order? Here's an order: Go up and get dressed. Take some money, and come back down here.

JULIE: Come up with me!

JEAN: To your room? You are mad. *(Hesitates, then)* No, now go!

(JEAN *takes* JULIE *by the hand and leads her out.*)

JULIE: Be nice to me.

JEAN: Orders always sound harsh. Now you know.

(JULIE *goes.* JEAN *sighs, sits at the table, takes out a notebook and pencil and counts aloud.* CHRISTINE *comes in, dressed for church. She carries a shirt-front and tie.*)

CHRISTINE: Look at this place. What have you been doing?

JEAN: Miss Julie dragged everyone in. You didn't hear anything?

CHRISTINE: I slept like a log.

JEAN: You're already dressed for church?

CHRISTINE: Aren't you coming with me? You promised.

JEAN: Those mine? Why not?

(CHRISTINE *helps* JEAN *put on the shirt and tie. Pause)*

JEAN: *(Sleepily)* What's the text today?

CHRISTINE: The beheading of John the Baptist.

JEAN: A long one. You're choking me. I can't keep my eyes open, I'm so sleepy.

CHRISTINE: What have you been doing all night? You look terrible.

JEAN: Sitting and talking with Miss Julie.

CHRISTINE: How dare she keep you up all night.

(Pause)

JEAN: Christine.

CHRISTINE: What?

JEAN: Funny, isn't it?

CHRISTINE: What is?

JEAN: Her. Everything.

(Pause. CHRISTINE *notices the half-empty glasses on the table.)*

CHRISTINE: And you've been drinking together.

JEAN: Yes.

CHRISTINE: And what else? Look at me.

JEAN: Yes.

CHRISTINE: It's not possible. That's not possible.

JEAN: Yes.

CHRISTINE: Oh God. How could you? I never would have dreamed—. How could you?!

JEAN: Jealous?

CHRISTINE: No. Not of her. If it'd been Clara or Sophie, I'd scratch your eyes out. But with her, it's different. I don't know why.

JEAN: Angry then?

CHRISTINE: At you. That was wrong. Poor girl. I can't stay here, I can't work for people I don't respect.

JEAN: Why do you need to respect them?

CHRISTINE: You think you're so smart. The people we serve, how they behave, reflects on us.

JEAN: Still it's nice to know they're no better than us.

CHRISTINE: I don't think so. If they're no better, then who's there for us to look up to? And think of the Count, all he's suffered. No, I can't stay in this house.

And to do it with someone like you. If it'd been the county attorney—one of our betters—.

JEAN: He isn't my—

CHRISTINE: Yes he is. He is. You're good enough, but there are different kinds of people. No, I won't be able to forget this. And she was so proud and standoffish with men. I'd have been surprised to see her touch a man, let alone give herself—and to a man like you. You know she wanted Diana shot because she was humped by the gate-keeper's mongrel. Who would have believed? Anyway, I'll leave, by October, I'll be gone.

JEAN: And then?

CHRISTINE: Since it's come up, you should start looking yourself. Since we're getting married.

JEAN: Look for what? I'd never even get a job as good as this, married.

CHRISTINE: No, you wouldn't. Maybe a janitor, a messenger in some government office. May not pay much, but it's steady, and there's a pension for the widow and children—.

JEAN: I can see what's in it for you, but I'm not quite ready to start dying yet. I have plans of my own.

CHRISTINE: What plans? You have responsibilities. Think of those.

JEAN: Don't lecture me. I know what I have to do, and I'll do it. *(Listens)* There's plenty of time to talk about this later. Get ready for church.

CHRISTINE: Who's walking up there?

JEAN: Clara?

CHRISTINE: It couldn't be the Count, could it? Maybe we didn't hear him come in.

JEAN: The Count! He would have rung.

CHRISTINE: *(Goes out)* Oh my God. What a mess this is.

(The sun has risen and shines on the tree tops in the garden. The light changes gradually until it comes in at a slant through the windows. JEAN goes to the door and gestures. JULIE enters dressed for travel and carrying a small bird cage covered with a cloth, which she places on a chair.)

JULIE: I'm ready now.

JEAN: Sh-sh. Christine's awake.

(JULIE shows signs of extreme nervousness during the scene.)

JULIE: Does she suspect anything?

JEAN: No. But look at you.

JULIE: What?

JEAN: You're as white as a ghost. What's on your face? Dirt?

JULIE: I better wash—. *(She goes to the washstand and washes her face and hands.)* Hand me a towel—. The sun! The sun's up!

JEAN: And so the monsters of the night are forced to scurry away.

JULIE: There were monsters here last night. Listen, Jean—I have the money. Enough. Come with me. I can't travel alone today, it's a holiday, the trains will be packed, with people staring at me. Interminable waits, when you just want to fly. I cannot. I can't. And the memories will flood back—of past midsummer holidays,the church turned forest with birches, lilacs. The dinner table with friends, relatives. The afternoon in the garden, music, dancing, flowers, games. One can fly, but your memories fly with you; they are your baggage stuffed with regret and remorse.

JEAN: I'll come, but only if we go now. Right now!

JULIE: Then get dressed. *(She picks up the cage.)*

JEAN: No baggage, it'll give us away.

JULIE: No—no baggage. Only what we can hold in our laps.

(JEAN has picked up his hat.)

JEAN: What is that?

JULIE: My bird. I can't leave it.

JEAN: Are you out of your mind? I'm supposed to drag around a bird cage? Leave it.

JULIE: It's all I'll take. It loves me. After Diana deserted me, it's all I had. Please let me take it.

JEAN: Leave the cage and be quiet. Christine will hear us.

JULIE: I'd rather see it dead than leave it with strangers.

JEAN: I can fix that.

JULIE: Be gentle. Don't hurt it. No, don't!

JEAN: Give it to me!

(JULIE takes the bird out of the cage and kisses it.)

JULIE: My little bird, must you die and leave me?

JEAN: It's only a damn bird. Your future's at stake. Your life. Quick, give it to me.

(JEAN snatches the bird, takes it to the chopping block, picks up an axe. JULIE turns away.)

JEAN: You should have been taught how to kill chickens, instead of how to shoot. *(Brings down the axe)* Then the sight of a little blood wouldn't be such a big thing.

JULIE: *(Screaming)* Kill me too! Kill me! You can butcher an innocent creature just like that! I hate you. I despise you. There's blood on your hands! I curse the moment

I set eyes on you. I curse the second I was conceived in my mother's womb!

JEAN: A lot of good cursing will do. Let's go.

JULIE: *(Approaching the dead bird)* No, I can't yet. Sh-sh. I hear a carriage. You think I can't stand the sight of blood? You think I'm weak. What I would give to see your blood, your brains on that block there. To see your whole sex swimming in blood like that thing there. I'd drink out of your skull, bathe my feet in your ripped open breast, eat your heart whole right off the spit! You think I'm weak? You think I love you because the fruit of my womb yearned for your seed? You think I want to carry your child under my heart, feed it with my blood? Bear it, and give it your name?
By the way, what is your name? I don't know it. I've never heard it. Perhaps you don't have any. Shall I become Mrs Peasant? Mrs Filth?
You there, dog, that's my collar you're wearing. You lackey, that's my coat of arms on your buttons. So I'm to eat off the same plate as my cook?! No, no, no! You think I'm afraid and will just run away? No, I'm staying now—and let's see what happens.
Father will come home—find his desk has been opened—money gone. He'll ring, ring again and then call the police. And I shall confess to everything. Everything. I can't wait to get this out. If only it ended there, but Father's heart will break, and he dies. And that is the end, the only end for any of us—peace, eternal rest. The coat of arms shattered over the coffin, the line broken, a family wiped out. While the dog's line continues in the orphanage, the gutter, the jail.

JEAN: Now your true self comes out. Bravo, Miss Julie. Now the cat's out of the bag.

(CHRISTINE enters with her prayer book. JULIE hurries to her and throws herself into her arms.)

JULIE: Help me, Christine. Help me!

CHRISTINE: *(Cold and unmoved)* It's Sunday morning. The Sabbath deserves better than this. *(Sees the chopping block)* What's been going on? What is all this shouting about?

JULIE: You're a woman. You're my friend. I warn you— he's a monster!

JEAN: While you girls talk, I'll shave. *(He goes.)*

JULIE: You must listen to me, listen to what I say.

CHRISTINE: Why should I? Aren't those your travel clothes? Was he wearing his hat?

JULIE: Listen, Christine, listen. I'll tell you everything—.

CHRISTINE: I don't want to know anything.

JULIE: Listen to me!

CHRISTINE: What?! About you and Jean? That's none of my business. But if he's running away with you—that I'll stop.

JULIE: Be quiet and listen. I can't stay here now and Jean can't stay here. So we have to leave.

CHRISTINE: I'm listening.

JULIE: But I have an idea! What if we all, say, went away—the three of us—together somewhere. To Switzerland—to start a hotel! I have money, see. Jean and I could run the whole thing and you—you could run the kitchen. It'll be so wonderful. Say yes, please, come with us—it'll fix everything—say yes!! *(She puts her arms around her.)*

CHRISTINE: I'm listening.

JULIE: You've never traveled, Christine. Seen the world! You'll love trains, they're so much fun, meeting new people, seeing new places—in Hamburg there's the zoo, we go through Hamburg, and there are the

theatres, the opera, Munich has museums, Rubens,
Raphael, all those famous painters, they're all there.
You've heard of Munich, King Louis lived there, King
Louis who went mad—. We can visit his palace—there
are palaces furnished exactly like they were hundreds
of years ago—and from there it's hardly any time
before we're in Switzerland, and those Alps, you know
them—they've got snow even in the summer, and
orange trees like moons and laurels, it's always green,
the whole year round—

(JEAN *is sharpening his razor on a strap which he holds
between his teeth and hand. He listens and every now and
then nods his approval.*)

JULIE: And then we get to the hotel—and I sit in the
office, Jean greets the guests—and does the shopping,
writes letters—that's the life, isn't it? The train whistles,
the buses drive up, it rings upstairs, it rings in the
restaurant—I better make up the bills—I'll pad them
too. You wouldn't believe how scared tourists are to
question anything! And you—you'll sit like a queen in
your kitchen. Not at the stove, God forbid. You'll have
nice clothes—guests will want to meet you—and with
your looks—I'm not just saying this—you'll hook a
husband in no time—some rich Englishman—they're
easy to catch—and we become rich and build a villa on
Lake Como—it's raining, it does that sometimes, but
the sun will come out—it will!—but it's dark now—
and—then—or maybe we just come home—come
back—here—or—wherever....

CHRISTINE: Miss Julie, is that what you really think will
happen?

JULIE: What I think will happen?

CHRISTINE: Yes.

JULIE: I don't know. I don't know what to think. *(She sinks down on the bench and holds her head in her hands.)* I know nothing. Nothing.

CHRISTINE: *(To* JEAN*)* So you were going to run off with her.

JEAN: Was I? I wouldn't put it that way. You've heard the plan. It could work.

CHRISTINE: And I'm to be that slut's cook?

JEAN: Don't you dare call her that. She's your mistress.

CHRISTINE: Mistress?

JEAN: Yes.

CHRISTINE: Listen to him.

JEAN: Yes, listen. What has she done that you haven't?

CHRISTINE: I have too much self-respect—.

JEAN: Self-regard.

CHRISTINE: To lower myself like that. Do I give myself to a field hand? Do I?!

JEAN: Only because you've been lucky enough to have someone like me.

CHRISTINE: Someone like you—who steals oats from the stable and resells them.

JEAN: What's that to you—who takes bribes from the butcher?

CHRISTINE: Who told you that?

JEAN: No, you—you're too good for your mistress.

CHRISTINE: Are you coming to church or not? You could use a good sermon.

JEAN: No, not today. You go—and confess your own sins.

CHRISTINE: I will, and I'll return with enough forgiveness for the both of us. Jesus suffered and died for our sins, we need only go to Him in faith and repentance to be forgiven.

JULIE: You really believe that?

CHRISTINE: It is everything I believe. And I have held to it since I was a child, Miss Julie. Where there is sin, there is God's grace.

JULIE: If only I had your faith.

CHRISTINE: But faith too is a gift from God. Some are chosen, some aren't.

JULIE: Who are the chosen?

CHRISTINE: That is a great mystery. Though we know that God cares not who people are. For Him the lowliest shall be first.

JULIE: Then he cares first for the lowliest?

CHRISTINE: *(Continuing)* It is easier for a camel to pass through the eye of a needle than for a rich man to enter the Kingdom of Heaven. That's the way it is, Miss Julie. Now I must go—alone. As I pass by the stable, I'll tell the boy not to let out any horses, I wouldn't want anyone getting away before the Count comes home. Goodbye. *(She goes.)*

JEAN: Bitch! All because of a damn bird!

JULIE: Forget the bird. What do we do?

JEAN: I don't know.

JULIE: What would you do, if you were me?

JEAN: If I were you? I don't know. The daughter of a Count. A woman who has…. You can't get it back. I don't know—no, I do know.

(JULIE picks up the razor and gestures across her throat.)

JULIE: Like this?

JEAN: Yes. Though it's not what I would do, myself. But then we come from different worlds.

JULIE: The different worlds of men and women? Is that what you mean?

JEAN: That too.

JULIE: *(With razor in hand)* I want to, but I can't. Like my father. He should have just done it.

JEAN: He still had something to live for—revenge.

JULIE: And now mother revenges herself again—through me.

JEAN: Don't you love your father, Miss Julie?

JULIE: With all my heart. Though I suppose I must hate him too—without even knowing it. He taught me to look down upon my sex. And look at me—half woman, half man! Who's to blame? Father? Mother? Me? I am nothing. Every thought I have is Father's, each passion Mother's, even the conviction that All Men Are Equal—this from my fiancé. How dare he put such thoughts into my head! So who's responsible for me?! Christine's Jesus? I have too much pride, I know too much, thanks to Father, to begin to do that. All that stuff about rich people and Heaven is just silly, even Christine must think so or she wouldn't be saving all her money in the bank. Who is responsible? Who cares? The truth is that I bear the guilt, and the punishment.

JEAN: Yes, but—.

(Two sharp rings of the bell. JULIE *is startled.* JEAN *changes his coat.)*

JEAN: The Count's—returned. Could Christine have—? *(Goes to the speaking tube. Into tube)* It's Jean, sir. *(Listens)* Yes, sir. *(Listens)* Yes, sir—right away. *(Listens)* It won't be a—. *(Listens)* Yes. In half in hour.

JULIE: What did he say? For God's sake, what did he say?

JEAN: He wants his boots. And then his coffee in half an hour.

JULIE: Half an hour it is then. I'm so tired. I can't move. I don't feel anything, I don't feel sorry, I can't run, I can't stay, I can't live—I can't die. Help me. Order me—I will obey like a dog. One last favor please—to save my honor, and save his name. I know what I should do, but I can't. Make me, make me do it!

JEAN: I can't—not anymore. I don't understand, I think it's the coat—putting it back on. I can't give orders to you. Just hearing the Count's voice—I'm a damned servant again—if he walked in here and told me to slit my own throat, I wouldn't be surprised if I did it—just like that.

JULIE: Then be him—and I'll be you. You're a good actor—you showed me this on your knees. Haven't you seen the hypnotist at the theater?

(JEAN *nods.*)

JULIE: He says to his subject: get the broom. And the man gets it. He says: sweep. The man sweeps.

JEAN: But the man is already asleep.

JULIE: *(Ecstatically)* And so am I! The room is full of smoke and you are the stove—tall and black like a man in a black suit and top hat. Your eyes glow like coals when the fire is dying. And your face a mound of white ash.

(The sunlight has reached the floor. It is now falling on JEAN.*)*

JULIE: Ah—it's so warm. *(She rubs her hands as if before a fire.)* And so light—and quiet.

(JEAN *takes the razor and puts it in* JULIE's *hand.*)

JEAN: Here's the broom. While it's light, go to the barn—and— *(He whispers in her ear.)*

JULIE: *(Awake)* Thank you. Now I will find rest. But tell me—for God shall the lowliest really come first? Tell me it's not true, even if you believe it is.

JEAN: I...I think there is some truth—but wait! Miss Julie you are now among the lowliest.

JULIE: That's true. I am among the lowliest. I am the last. Why can't I go? Help me!

JEAN: I can't. I can't help!

JULIE: And those above us—let them be last.

JEAN: Don't think! Don't think! You're sapping my strength! What's that? I thought I heard a bell! No. Scared of a bell. No, not of the bell—but of what's behind it, the hand that rings it, and of what's behind the hand. Cover your ears! Cover them! But it rings louder! Rings and rings until you answer. And then it's too late—and then it's the police—and then....

(Two quick rings of the bell. JEAN *nearly collapses, then straightens himself up.)*

JEAN: I'm sorry. But what can I do? Go!!!

*(*JULIE *goes out through the door.)*

END OF PLAY